Staying Amazed

———— with ————

God

LARRY CUMMINS

Larry Cummins (signature)

ISBN 978-1-63844-845-7 (paperback)
ISBN 978-1-63844-846-4 (digital)

Christian Faith Publishing, Inc.
832 Park Avenue
Meadville, PA 16335
www.christianfaithpublishing.com

Printed in the United States of America

Point of Release

On bended knee, I find peace. So sweet it won't stop. I'm in the glory so heavy.

I can't stand.

Holy Spirit speaks to me in a very familiar voice.

"I love you, my child. You serve me well.

"I know your pain. Let me take it. I will crush it and send it to the abyss.

"That old trickster can't win. He chases you like a cat chases his tail.

"He can't win. I send you so much power and love. He does not want to be next to you."

Praise the Father and the Son. True victory! Amen.

All Alone

Hear what I hear. It is complete silence flowing through my whole body.

It seems dark and alone. I listen for a sound. I hear it. It's a leaf falling.

That's how isolated alone is.

When I pray, no Spirit is talking in my ear. I can't determine why I am alone. Suddenly, God speaks to me.

"Don't fear, child! I am here even if you don't hear me.

"I am here even if you can't see me. You're never alone. Cry out, and I will stop to hear you stand with your faith. Open your heart and celebrate your soul."

When the Spirit Calls

The voice in my ear is the spirit of God.

"Rest to grow in my love.

"Call out to search the unknown. I will teach you I am the spirit of God.

"Go to my Word, which is alive with mysteries. Seek what I tell you so you can conduct my will. When the river runs through your soul, I will cleanse your heart white as snow.

"My blood is fully capable of healing your wounds. Walk with me. I am the comforter. Peace is real. I'll send it in the form of a gift. Hear my voice so sweet and soft, sounding like love. It's my Spirit calling to you. Just say yes."

Ask with Your Eyes

I look in your eyes. I see your pain. It's alive with torment.

I ask the master to take it. Such strongholds. The darkness is shot through your soul. Jesus, please—my God, lose this pain. He said, "I know.

"I will love you back to sanity. That torment is in no way yours. The enemy wants you dead. I give you life abundantly, freely.

"You will have no scars, no trauma. Sleep in your soul. Let my Holy Spirit bring you comfort, peace, freedom, and praise. Ask with your eyes."

First Things First

Look at what is first in the heart of the heavenly Father. First, love me with all your heart, mind, and soul. Give your whole self to Jesus. Open your heart and ask to be reborn in the Spirit. Shed yourself to be made whole. Seek ye first the kingdom of God. Live in the light of heavenly host and receive a double portion. Let God create in you what you can't. Open your mind, heart, and soul to do his will in your life. Reach to the Father's hands. Be healed, be strong, be able to speak truth with destiny. No more helplessness. Holy Ghost power, you are free.

Fractures of the Spirit

O Father God, look at my spirit. It's so fractured. How can I know your love when I'm so blocked and trapped in these fractures?

It's like being in the dark spot, lost and alone. I cried out to your Holy Spirit and asked for comfort. You are so faithful! Suddenly, I felt relief in my spirit. Healing has begun.

Expose to me all the hidden places in my fractures that are so powerful over me. I know that a ransom was paid and Jesus released me into a new freedom. I celebrate my salvation, which makes me a new creation. Love lays over these fractures. The same love Jesus has for us.

Peace Beyond

Peace that surpasses all understanding. It comes in the form of love.

You cannot explain it. You can't stop it. It travels through your soul like cool water on a hot day. Like a breeze in the meadow on a mountain.

I feel it when angels flutter their wings—there is a calming sense of well-being. Like a newborn being held by his mother. Such strength in this quiet place. Look to God for my joy never-ending. Nothing can steal it if it comes from him.

Reaching the Limitless

Go ahead and look at the impossible. For a moment or two, you may be set back.

Lift your eyes to heaven; let your spirit soar with faith. Get filled with limitless power and touch the angels' wings. If you're undone and can't function, the Holy Spirit can cause you to reach the limitless love of Christ. The reach of his heart is so huge that we cannot conceive its glorious, peaceful power. Words are limitless. No more powerlessness. Search the storehouse of the mind of Christ.

He heals my thoughts so I can deliver limitless love. No conditions.

Your Emotions

Trust in God, not my emotions. Hurt is real no matter how long it lasts. God gives us real noise in our ears. The enemy wants us dead. Search your heart—there is no end. God knows our heart like he knows our breath. I have to know the reason to let go. Fever in my soul, boil the pain—let it go. Don't stop now. I push the limit on pain. Go now, and let it go. Shame and guilt are gone. Let me save this in the record book. To you, God, I owe my heart and wholeness. There is a way out of the torment: the great comforter—the Holy Spirit.

The Lamb and the Lion

Eyes wide open. There's a gentle spirit in the room. Prayers are spoken, and peace enters in search of your quiet place. Has the Lamb of God touched your soul? The vision comes with rapid movement. In my heart, the lion is roaring. He wants to speak with authority, but no one can hear. The Holy Spirit has the power to make things clear. Suddenly, I feel a tear run down my cheek. Not sad, not happy. But submitted to the power and mercy of God. Let loose. Don't hold on. Be free. No more lion. The Lamb rules the beast.

Rarely to Fail

When I wake to the morning, I rarely fail to contact my precious Jesus. He's always waiting, eyes wide open. Ears listening to my woes.

"Let me love you and free you from this lie you have been believing. Search your heart so I, the Lord God, can heal you of your losses. No longer are you a prisoner to sin. It will come and go. However, it won't own you. Stay on the path to reality.

"Let no man say, 'Heal not.' Just the opposite. Go to God, and let him heal."

Amen.

Quick to Love

Be slow to anger and quick to love. It is love that releases all my chains. Even where I'm locked up in chains, love can set me free. Love is the power. It beholds all creation in a moment. The power of Christ's love—that glorious ransom he paid. Those scars paid a debt I couldn't pay. He speaks love through his great pain. He shouts, "I love you, Father!"

Did not question his Father's love. Faith reigns over my brain. Do these things with the intentions of love. It permeates my DNA. You, Father God, make that forgiveness possible. Touch me and my spirit so it can speak at a new level.

Enter My World

My voice is untamable; my breath is like the wind in the lilies. You don't have to push to receive it. My power is yours endlessly. I heal you. I comfort you, so rejoice! To the world, I am yours, and you are mine.

Speak to me. I will listen. I will talk to you. Words that teach you my will. I am the God of reason. I will kick away the stone. There are no limits to my omnipresence. My love for you is great.

Seek to Please the Father

So they went to the holy places of good peoples' hearts. Sent by assignment to release the unknown. Seeking only love as a gift, one person to the next. Shuffle the voice of God through the filter of your heart. Take a risk to be wrong or right. Rest with comfort with the Holy Spirit. He can comfort your troubles. Do not own the flaws the enemy has tried to attach to you. You were born again—no longer a child of Satan. You're now a child of God. Let his power, grace, and mercy control all of you, not just part of you. Seek to please the Father.

Rest in My Arms

Go to the quiet place. I will be there waiting for you. Reach to your inner self, and give to me your pain. Give to me your confusion. Give to me your blindness. I will send to you healing balm from my arms. When they wrap around you, it will be life-changing. You will have peace. You will have sight. My Holy Spirit will cause you to dance and sing. The joy of the Father's presence will release your spirit to the supernatural. The power I give you will be new, so be prepared to get full of my Spirit. No limitations.

Stranger to Stranger

They passed in the night. It was pitch-black, yet their eyes were aglow. It's as if they were tiny torches lighting up the darkness. When one spoke, he had a story to tell.

"My God, he healed me when I should have been dead."

It sent shivers down my spine. I knew it was the spirit of God upon both of us. I asked if the encounter with God had changed his life, and he resounded with a smile from deep within. The choice was mine just like now; we are no longer strangers. We are now friends touched by God's love. We must grow and pass again.

Executing Vision

My mind is in God's hands. Free from fear even if it comes. I won't let fear define me. There's always something bigger God wants me to do. I don't want to be seventy-three doing what God wanted me to do at twenty-six. Don't be comfortable—do what the Holy Spirit wants you to do! Don't wait for your miracle. Speak it! Live in the ridiculousness of God's grace. He will always display enough to deliver his glory. God is good. He gives us joy. God's promises are real. He cannot lie. He's provoked by love and random kindness. He will deliver you from your iniquities.

Walking Near the Edge

You're sent to hover in dark places. Seek your needs in my power. Rest in my arms. Soak in my Holy Spirit. You will be the substance of my blood on your flesh. The evil one will run in your thoughts. You're not trapped. You're free to glide like a kite in the air. I will save your praise. Go to the beginning of your place. I have chosen you for a specific need of mine. You are a heavenly design. Give to your prethoughts my Spirit. Join with me all of your shortcomings. I will make you perfect. My will be done. Glory, honor, power, and peace. No darkness—only light and joy. My love is for all. No one is exempt. Shh, I quiet your spirit to hear my Holy Spirit, and joy shall stand tall, uninterrupted. I, the Lord God, say it's your turn to prevail. Your war cry will not go unheard. I, the Lord God, place you in the right place and in the right time with the right gifts.

Everything God Has

I look around on this earth. I see all is God-given. Trees are permanent. Wind is motion. Rain is water of life. Everything God has made is holy. God's holiness includes all; only man can exclude the Father. Testify to God, the Son, and the Holy Spirit; spirit, soul, and body are integrated and led by the spirit of God. Don't let your emotions go out of control. God Almighty makes me one with integrity and trust in the Lord. This begins with repeated reality. The Word of God can't lie, so he has made for himself a name: Jesus Christ. Come to him in Jesus's name. God the Father knows I'm integrated.

What Is Old May Pass—I Will Not

Send to me what is new so I remember the old. Release healing to my fractures untold. Open my captivated pain. I must let go into your arms. Warm my heart so I can see freedom and not loss. Grow my spirit closer to your Holy Spirit. Open my unrevealed places to speak loudly into the heavens to shift the angels with praise. Settle the unshakable. Put up the pillars of strength. Hold me tight. Don't let go. I know you will not change. You will not lie. Your promises are real. Healings, anointing, gifting, and miracles—they are very real. I will not pass or go away. Eternity lives.

Altered

Look to what is. No servant can see a restful need. Maybe it will come to you: blind emotion in God. Your spirit can alter your actions. Search the power plant of your heart. Plead to the heavenly Father to release his grace and mercy on you. Open your eyes to receive this sight. Undo your hearing of the word *interpretations*. Interpretations will be quick and true. Eagles will fly by, ready to defend God's angels. The enemy will flee then stop. Take what is yours because I, the living God Almighty, have released in you a heavenly touch so powerful that it cannot be described.

Glory to the Almighty

My ears are flooded with stories from the heavenly places. I reach heights of new beginnings with the contrast of the old. God the Almighty shifts my strengths to his power and grace. Search the heart of God and release the untold secrets of his holiness. Let the rain fall on your skin so you can know he is the temperament of love and obedience. The Lamb of God chooses to love you and heal all of your human voids. Rest your thoughts in his grace. His mercy. His strong arms loose in me the tolerance high in his glory. All praise to the Father.

I Love Your Presence

Feel you, touch you, hear you. Let me know how to love you. Let me know how to feel you. Let me know how to hear you. I will be obedient to your Word. Release me to worship in your being so your power will overtake the place we can't give to you. Fire up your willingness. Push my spirit to new heights. Position me to commit your will in this place. With your power and your will, let the angels dance without reserve. It's all about the power he uses to make us stand tall. The looking glass must be cleared.

Peace Interactive

I feel your peace—your mighty peace. It isn't starved. It settles my soul. My shortcomings are washed by your blood. Teach me to receive your perfect glory. Be full of joy, lost in your spirit. No limits to guide me. Seize my spirit and cause it to soar like the eagle. Spread angel wings over me. By your stripes, I am healed and made whole. Let the past die to live new, fully in your presence. Let the harp sound to gleeful ears. Know how to blink. Let me dwell in you. "You will know I am God."

Ending Pain

Touch the master with the heartbeat of your soul. Feel the lightning crackle at the crushing pain. The Holy Spirit will penetrate like water, soothing the nerves like sweet, homemade jelly on fresh bread. Comfort like a warm blanket soothes the newborn. Jesus, heal my pain. Take it to the cross. Leave it there, never to return. Let me speak with faith and testimony. The living God does have the power to end all pain. God delivers in the realm of all. Praise his holy name.

Speak Truce and Surrender

Let the words come from your soul. Lest you fight the lift of your spirit. Lay down the fight against God's Spirit of open heaven's highway. Let it lead you in truth, glory, and honor. Seek the Son in all his power to heal your bleeding. Identify the crushing blows that you took. Let them fall. The Holy Spirit is going to chase you. Don't lose your human weakness and transform your spiritual well-being. Angels can rejoice in your actions. Seek truce. Ask his grace to teach your spirit to celebrate your glory to the end.

Glory to Glory

We travel in the Spirit to be taught by the grace of God. Search the night in your dreams for the truth in vision. Destroy the enemy's strongholds. His clutches must release you through God's glory. Open your heart to glory. God breathes life into you. Don't back down—celebrate your glory! Rejoice in his name. Jesus Christ will empower you to do battle. Loose that which is bound. Nothing can separate you from God. Not even your own thoughts. Go glory to glory. Build strong bridges to hold any amount of weight. Just remember, God will always love you.

Tears with Meaning

You stand in the shadows looking in, paralyzed from fear. Now you hear the Lord of all Lords calling you. Your spirit tells you to respond. However, the bondage is so real the Lord says, "Fear not, child of mine."

And the enemy says, "You're stuck. You are mine."

Suddenly, tears begin to flow. It's as if they are healing my pain.

"Listen to me, child. The evil one does not own you. Even in your state of unforgiveness, I release this bondage. Freedom is now yours! The tears you cried have great meaning."

Unknown Destiny

Walking for a while, looking for my truth. God speaks and tells me, "I am the truth you seek."

Dear God, what is it you shall have me do? The Holy Spirit searches my heart to check my motives. They come from you. I don't know my destiny; however, I will search the unknown. I feel your love in my life every day. I just don't know what you want me to do, God. Please reveal to me the unknown destiny for your will in my life. Cause me to reveal any hidden agendas that I have. Keep me searching your everlasting love.

Seek the Opening

Walking in a field, I saw an opening in the sky. Angels came down to walk with me. I felt a peace inside. To what extent are you here? To deliver me into light?

Fill the darkness with love and light going in a perfect direction, looking to God the Father as an everlasting life.

Thank you, Jesus. There is such a delight in your love! I can see the intensity of love in your eyes going to the innermost part of my being. When I am lost and don't know what to do, your love gives me direction to be free.

No bondage!

Delightful Noise

I hear the praise on your lips—so refreshing. When you speak my name, it is a release of perfect peace. The noise I hear is not a clanging symbol but music of praise. Let it continue to my angels for they record it for me to hear. The portals of heaven are open from praise coming from your lips. Surrender that which is mine to me by loving me and giving me all of you. Be bold with your prayers. Teach praise with your lips. Bend your knee to accept my power and glory. Clarity for this is you in my presence.

Facing Fear

Yeah, though I walk in fear, God will release in me his Holy Spirit to empower me to take authority over evil. When Jesus in me delivers light in me, all darkness must leave. Eye to eye with the enemy, Jesus in me takes victory over and crushes my enemy. Face everything and roar like a lion! Father God, please send me courage to face this fear. I'm in a spiritual battle for strength. From glory to glory, Jesus, please carry me.

Peace and Grace

Peace to you rounded with the words from the Most High. Holy Spirit, you are the most of all on earth. Grace is unmerited, bound by wild desire. I feel your Spirit take over because I can't create without you, God. Little do I have alone. God, hold me planted in your arms, please. There is no torment! Reveal to me your will; loose me, rattle my free will. Close to you, I dance to the pace of love.

Don't stop!

Surely

My child, it is I who stitched the beauty into the sky. It is I who made mankind in my image. So put your fears away; rest in the heart of God the Father for surely I have not forsaken you! Your shortcomings are but a silk purse with my DNA on them. Rejoice and be glad in all things forever! Glory to glory, my power is pure without flaw. So put your dependency in my hands. Your fractures are for me to heal. Also, I heal your wounds. Stop all bleeding; I hear your heart's cry. I, the Lord God, will produce in you a love so powerful it will be realized as mine.

Real Pain

Your pain is real my child. So I give you the ability to feel it. My power and grace will cause your eyes to cry tears of joy, not sorrow. Empty your emotions into my new wine skin. It will hold them. I will carry you the distance of the map as it appears on your heart. Do not fear; rather, love with all your being. Rush to the mountaintop and scream my name. All my creation will hear your cry. I am God. I make all things possible. Peace is at hand.

Love.
Learn.
Test.
Stitch.
Search.
Live.

Firmly Planted

Don't go away to leave. Let me heal you! Don't send a message of negative report. Hold the wings of angels—let them fly! Search your heart to its fullest growth. Live life on life's terms with Jesus, the creator of your freedom. Sense the gifts so freely given; use them to their fullest. Search out the broken and heal them. Find the lost and direct them. It is Jesus who says, "I love you no matter what."

You are not locked up. God is not in a box.

Hurt for You

Let me take your hurt. See through my heart into love; I alone hurt for you. Let me love you until you can love yourself. Peace is available to your inner being through my Holy Spirit. Celebrate the gifts I have released to you. Know I am present to hurt for you. Let me deliver you out of your oppression. Seek me on your face—I will deliver you from your hurt. I have made it my own. Just speak it out to me; I am faithful to heal.

Grace

It is so wonderful to know about your grace. To be fallible and still receive grace is so incredible! Searching for grace is such a small act. I can never pay the price for your great love for me. Nor can I duplicate what grace covers even in your unrevealed secrets, dark and crushing. Yet still, grace—your grace—is sufficient to heal and free my spirit. Please open the channel of grace all the way to my soul. I love you.

Jesus Is Alive

I am Jesus. Let me speak to you. Let me share my gifts with you. Let the pupils of your eyes open the door to the next dimension. Let my nail-scarred hands heal you and make you whole. I am the supernatural power for you to use for deliverance. My blood heals addiction, cancer, and the like. Raise your faith—let me give you what you don't deserve. Let me take the enemy out. I am a very large God. Let me be bigger than you. I'll stand before you and reveal my grace to you. It will flow through your veins. You are in process. Every one of you is my success. Praise my name! Serve the Holy Spirit; speak truth and life with my almighty word. The gospel shall spread throughout the land. Be a part of my bride, the church. Love, live, and teach people about Jesus.

Unspoken

My thoughts are many, filled with unknown resolve. Take my thought life to a higher plane. Search my motives for vain imagination. Let my brain waves carry the very thoughts of the Holy Spirit. To harm is so irreversible. Help me to never harm. Emotions are powerful, but not in control. Jesus is in control. What is not spoken is still known. To see God's will takes willingness to be humble enough to hear. Prayer is the avenue to God's will. Listen, look, and learn what God wants. Very unspoken, he will reveal it.

Shadows in the Cracks

I'm filled with shadows in the cracks of my spirit. Dear heavenly Father, heal my brokenness; let it be freed to do your bidding. Some tall, some short. I can't seem to sort them out. Stretch the cracks. Open them up. Be rid of these hiding places called shadows. Don't let the pain grow. End it in your holy name. Blanket the bleeding—stop it. Let healing take over on a real level. Bring me out of the shadows with no open wounds. Please, Father God, stop the bleeding. Light up the shadows so they are gone. Nowhere to hide. Amen.

Praise Is Clear

Praise to the Father who directs the angels. Release to me flowing words of praise. Lift my spirit, O Lord. Hear my voice. Suddenly, I can reach new levels of spirituality. Jesus, you are so present; the Holy Spirit is so alive. I'm dancing like a child in the park. I scream, I sing, and I moan, speaking in heavenly song. It gives me goosebumps on my goosebumps. Love is the sweet touch of gifts. Can you see it? Live and learn to open your mouth to let it be known. How your heart floods with sweet praise not to be held back lest you let the enemy in. Praise! Chase him out! Let God in! He can shout healing, peace, truth, release, and DELIVERANCE!

Hear My Voice

Though you may be young and very small, don't let that send you to nowhere. "Hope is mine," sayeth the Lord.

"Look to my face and let my power give you joy. I'll teach you about my voice. It is stitched into your spirit. When I made you, I put it there. You can release it for my glory. Jesus is taught by my love and power. Believe that I will free you from your captivity. Search your innermost spirit, and my will shall come out. To you I gave free will to have joy. Search that love out and hold onto it and learn to give it away. Lean into me; I will wipe clean the lenses in your eyes so you can see me. I can give you peace beyond your reasoning. No wave in the water. Calm the sea. I will love you, my child."

Jewels

Glowing in the dark with great brightness. When your spirit touches me, I'm glowing. I feel like a jewel never touched before. With clarity and accented edges, I can't be duplicated. I'm one of a kind! Glory to God on most high. He loves me and paid the ransom on my soul with his blood on that cross. Jewels are gifts that sparkle and glow. I'm a gift from God to mankind. Let his love empower me to live up to that jewel status. Shout to the Holy Spirit. Love is at hand. So much love—pure love—no conditions.

And God Winked

I said, "God, I got this, no problem."

And God winked. "Let me send power to you," and God winked because he knew I would run. I cried for help, and God answered. He didn't wink when I removed myself. I searched other wisdom for myself, and God winked. "Hold fast, my child. My wisdom will direct your footsteps."

"Hey, God, I'm going to climb this mountain!"

And God winked as it began to snow. I think my actions are mostly selfish, and God winked. Just loves unconditionally. "My grace is far and wide. Reach its perimeter."

Shadow Darkness

I'm resting in the darkness of familiarity. So much shadow between the light. Defects are profound; no good stands out. Suddenly the light takes over. I'm all lit up! How can it be? God loves me. Enough to give me hope. I'm lost, not to be found. So comfortable in my broken shadow. I cried in the light; my spirit knew it was you, God, who loved me back out of the shadow of darkness. Never could rejoice in love and truth until your Spirit came and comforted me back to life. No more darkness, only light.

Holy Fire

Free me from all hesitations; burn in me a holy fire to release your mercy. Send your holy fire to heal my iniquities. Let the enemy's lies fall to the ground and turn to dust. Let us enter his camp and take back what he has stolen. Sweet holy fire, speak to the core of my being. Let your hand touch my brokenness and seam it with golden thread from your hair and let your angels rejoice and speak to us. Sing praise to the living God.

And the holy fire roars like the mighty lion.

True Believers

I believe in you, Jesus. I trust in you. Make me a true believer. Reform my spirit; let it be new. Send your power and grace to open my eyes to see what you see, hear what you hear. Remove all unholiness that is not of you. Bring me into your spirit and cause me to be a true believer. Help me not to stutter. Speak with tongues not my own—only heaven can know. The enemy can't operate in that true belief of heaven. No darkness, bring light. Rest not in the flesh. Seek true motives that show and prove love.

The Comforter

I know the spirit of God is my comforter, living to love and to be loved. Searching my heart for trueness, no dismay. I am settled in the very power of the Holy Spirit. It fills the room with a sweet fragrance. It calms the shaking nerves. I lust after God's will for my life. It brings light to my eyes. Dark shadows are illuminated to brightness. Hush my difficulties so the enemy must flee. My spirit inside is alive with compassion for my fellow man. Let me love more.

On the Bridge

On the bridge over the sea of forgetfulness, standing with Jesus I am. I come to the cross daily, and Jesus's blood washes me clean. There in the sea of forgetfulness on the bridge, I can see what Jesus has done for me. Don't wonder but believe that Jesus alone can give you freedom. No matter how broken you are, he can heal you and deliver you from your bondage. Joy is at hand while on that bridge. Over the sea, Jesus installed joy and peace. All torment gone. "I instruct you to love like me in whole spirit. Release my gifts to others."

No Name

Even if I had no name, God would still know me. He created me. He knew me before I was in my mother's womb. My identity is not held in my issues. I'm released, healed, and holy even with no name! Pray to seek. Speak to affect others. Love will name me with the power of the Holy Spirit. Rest in my faith. Let God reveal to me my identity. Pain becomes past. Not to last. It's no longer attached to my identity—now my identity is in Christ. No more tears. Just love.

Bring Me to Your Heart, Lord

When I pray, stand with me. Wrap your endless love around me. Bring me to your heart. Release your love upon me so I may deliver it to the whole world. Open my heart, Lord, so I can see what you see.

Set my soul in your ways. Reach my heart, Lord; heal my unknowing. Reveal the inability to go with your will. You walk with me in my weakness and bring me to humility.

Suddenly I cried, "Bring me to your heart, Lord. Let me feel it beat as the glory falls. Health is the promise of faith. Shudder my emotions. Bring me to your heart, Lord. Settle it in my spirit."

Sweet Peace

The Holy Spirit brings sweet peace to me. Rest in the sunset. I give you every good thing like pure honey and fresh fruit and sweet peace. No more suffering. Rest your torment in my sweet peace. Blink your eyes in darkness. I will rid you of the shadows of your enemies with sweet peace. Your grace can be tasted and savored like sweet peace. Wars and rumors of wars are ended by great peacemakers who are lovers of my sweet peace. Flow in my praise and Spirit.

The Source

I bring streams into the desert. I grow a new thing with my hand. Give me your trust. Go about our Father's business with the Holy Spirit. We are united! Shout it from the mountains; sing it with your voice and your worship. Dance in love with my love. The river in you is me. Celebrate my glory. Give it to me. I will give beyond your reason. I created you to serve me. I give you things you can't create. Be grateful like a babe on a bottle. It satisfies your needs. Let it happen.

Set in His Mind

Before you were born, you were on his mind. Set in your ways. Dying, you were on his mind. Nowhere to go, you were on his mind. Living on the streets, you were on his mind. When you were abused, you were on his mind. When you were separated from your family, you were on his mind. When you served the king alcohol, you were on his mind. When you went to war, he was on your mind. When you were there, you were on his mind. Now I'm at the bottom, and you are on my mind. Jesus, I humbly ask, please forgive me!

To Love

To love in the direction of Jesus, put in place a want to serve in love. Pace the intolerance of my mind to love in my heart. Connect my eyes to see love. Open my ears to hear in love and praises to heavenly places. Ask to love freely. Receive love so you can give it away. Jesus presented love freely, never saying if or when. He merely said, "Now I love you."

To love goes the request. Free my heart; set it loose to love in your power and grace. Wring out the evil in me. Replace it with love.

Spiritual Form

That which is esteemed in men is an abomination! My form is shaped by the word of God. Let the gifts of the Holy Spirit transcend from heaven. Grant me godly wisdom to share the endless growth in me. Let my spiritual form grow with a heavenly voice. Shout with praise. Let glory reign to its fullest. Any spiritual form from God is called to send the message of the gospel. Remove doubt. Have a holy moment. Come to the master, God of all Gods. Let it soar like the mighty eagle. Rest in your spiritual form.

Lasting Beyond Pain

I start pain as a normal activity. Suddenly I am asking: Is this right? Am I hurting to be who I am? Look deeper to find the answer you seek. There are parables not yet revealed that a mere mortal man cannot comprehend. God will constantly reveal more to us and others.

Peace comes with a price. Go to the center of the heart to see if it is truly broken. Holy Spirit can redesign the heart seamlessly. Let it feel joy unspeakable. If you grow weary, release to the Father your weakness. He alone will empower you to last beyond the pain!

I Know It's Your Breath

I'm sitting quietly, listening to the leaves move, and I know it's your breath blowing on them. I see the wind like I see you. I first have to have faith to believe. Then I recognize the evidence that it's you who cleared the wind. I see the clouds move in the sky again, looking through your eyes. When I am walking alone in the forest, I feel your breath pass through me. Such a peaceful feeling. Now I know it's your breath. Deep breath in after I should have been dead. I know it's the breath of God. When I see the eagle fly, it has to be God's breath.

Go ahead. Breathe.

Pour Out on the Water

Look at my being on the water. I can take your only loss. Turn to me to your touch. Let your power infiltrate me with no resistance. The course of our healing is perfect. Shall I love like you? Shall I see like you? Open divine peace in your loving arms. I feel the safety of your compassion. I press into your Spirit. The Holy Spirit gives me comfort and joy. I'm no longer blinded by the enemy. Open my body to your sacrifice. The ransom has been paid by the son, Jesus Christ.

Real Thoughts

Who's in the hallway of my mind? Is it fear?

Who controls my mind? Hear God's voice, not the spirit of fear. Cast out fear and negativity! Spirit of love and sound mind abound. God has a dream, and the power of God creates holy fire. Erase the bad thoughts in my mind. Change the structure of my mind. No hopelessness nor fear. Renew my mind. Beauty for ashes in the river can carry my defects away. They do not create my destiny. The mind of God for nations leads all my people to me. He alone controls the universe.

Wanting More

Searching my heart, I want more. There's a care in my heart. I'm not lost, but I am being touched by a power. It leaves me wanting more. Can this even be satisfied? I pray to Jesus to let me love. Help me see the solid, unavoidable love that permeates my soul. No hesitations in my mind. Only the will of the Father. Rest in glory. Be washed in grace! No enemy can win. His heart leaves me wanting more.

Grace Extended

It's what changes before our very eyes. When we can't change—or won't—God delivers us out of the darkness. My very core is rocked when Jesus speaks in his word. Things like value are not cheap. Send it to the highway; grace is always honored. I can't achieve it. Drop to your knees; get God into your core. The angels are speaking to report to the Father. If we have a need that's not being met, speak to it and say, "God is the lover of my soul!"

Feast to Live On

Check in to Jesus so he can hear your motives. Look to the mountaintops and shout, "Jesus, I love you! Let me follow you so I become a lover of your presence! Loose me like the treetops in the wind! Create a worship on my lips that causes the enemy to stop."

We must trust in God the Father for his power to drive our authority. Open our spirits to feast on spiritual love so great that we cannot stand in the glory. His holiness is upon us, shifting all our thoughts to feast.

Enter In

My Spirit is always there. Touch your soul. Open the passage to your belly. Cry out to me; I alone will satisfy you. When you are hungry, I will feed you. Believe what I tell you; it is the truth. I will wash you through and through and remove the fear from your heart. Send me your brokenness. If you know me, you will know my Father. Touch my garment. Be healed. The Father only knows truth to release you from your bondage. Bright light experience shines on you.

Seated in Glory

Rush to the place for you to meet with God the Father. His glory will overcome your spirit if you allow it. Take the gift of glory; rest with it in your soul. You will not lose any status by being seated in glory. Praise will fall off your tongue never heard before. Just know, when you know the Son, the Father God seats you in glory. His pain and stripes paid the ransom for our souls. Cry out—say the things you need to say. He will honor you to the end of all time. Hold your hand in his. Feel the nail scars. Yes, you are my child seated in glory.

Deliver to Me Compassion

Receive the very same compassion Christ had on the cross. For he died for all of God's creation. He said no to Satan when he offered him this planet. Because he knew the Father had compassion and he would be that eternal compassion. Send to me that transfer of true love so I may, through you, look in other peoples' eyes and sense the need for that Christlike compassion. Calm the raging storm within. Open the windows of their souls. Rest in your glory and goodness. How powerful that is! It is a dance.

Loaded with Love

The pulse in my heart seemed empty. Darkness was present. I cried out to God to please remove this pain so deep. Then suddenly, light appeared to dispel the darkness. The pulse shifted to life so completely. No more emptiness. Let me feel your Holy Spirit in my gaps filling my soul. Now complete holiness and oneness with Jesus as he loves on me soaring like eagles in the updraft. My heart beats strong and completely. No limits on this love. Restful peace rolling off the tears as they turn to laughter, telling the complete story of love.

Tears

Tears flooded from my eyes. They seem to hold unspeakable joy. Backed by the power of love. Jesus, behold. My spirit lives in your glory. Powered by your grace. No tears of sadness. Even if I am broken, you still say I am yours. How could that be except for grace! Dark tears—no one can see them except Jesus. Your love is so sweet. Light consumes everybody's pain. Eternal life is greatness created by God. Let Jesus split you away from your pain. He will make you whole. Praise to God.

Peace Directed

John 14:27

Reach for Jesus to be directed by God's love never-ending. Peace shall flow like a waterfall spreading and directing his will with glory. Be on an endless journey of grace and love. Be quick to shout, "Heavenly Father of love!"

Peace directed by his love is unstoppable, blessed by glory risen by his power. Angels flutter their wings and cause the demons to flee. My peace travels to the very reaches of the entire universe. This peace speaks all the love any creature is capable, delivering peace directed by your glorious power eternal.

My Rain

My rain births the angels' fire and power. Let go of your worldly devastation. Give me your trust; stimulate the fire of my power. Seek out the enemy and his camp. Destroy it with my overwhelming love. When my Spirit flows, everything stops to listen. You cannot deny it. It is not jungle babble. It's clear just like raindrops and dew on the leaves. I will take charge of my people in the end. I, GOD, will reign for eternity!

Fortitude

When facing difficulty, we are able to encounter danger or bear pain, both emotional and physical. The Holy Spirit does not waver! We display great levels of bravery and calmness that create emotional power with strength to crush the enemy. We endure evil and see things from God's perspective. It is a true gift. The knowledge stays in your mind. While praying, open the heart and let your Holy Spirit fortitude completely empower me to do your will.

Sounds of Power

Listen to my sounds from the wind. Your heartbeat is equal to my love in process. No whisper too low. Speak with power and grace. Angel wings create noise to vibrate the Holy Spirit. Your prayers are the sound of power. Release your weakness so I can empower you to live inside of the living Christ. Go with trust and faith to be used by the hand of God. Move in signs and wonders. The sound of power is love. Impart it to the world!

Prepare Your Heart

Look to the Lord of all Lords. Roll in peace to prepare your heart. Father of mine, send your glory down on my heart. Let it beat to your will. There's no way to hide your love in my heart. It bleeds your compassion. Open the vessels of my heart. Each chamber is overfull with your love. Don't stop there. Let it burst in your favor on all of your kingdom. Lay down my old ideas so you can send the holy reign forever serving you, O Father God.

Angels on High

An army exists on high to protect and serve my people. Some to love, some so big they tower over the weak. Some so powerful they carry my healing heart. High above to see your needs of protection. Don't worry. Trust even if you don't see them; they are there. Then the angels of praise open my portals to pour out my Holy Spirit on you. They move all around you in the air high above you. They serve the mighty God operating in his mercy.

The Morning Dew

I war with you in the morning dew. Tell me your troubles as you walk. Wash your face with that clean dew moisture. I will cleanse your mind and enter into your place of worship to me. Where you are is where I am also. You bend to my Holy Spirit, surrender to the sound of peace in my presence. Let me be the perfection of the morning dew on tall grass in a high mountain field. Wings of my angels blow my favor on your spirit. Lose any restrictions on your spirit.

Heaven to Earth

It is my glory on your face. Do not doubt it. Feel the light of the sun and the moon. That's heaven to earth. A bird's wings carry wind and flight. That's heaven to earth. The blind is made to see. That's heaven to earth. A young child with a death sentence is healed from cancer. That's heaven to earth. My Holy Spirit directs angels on assignment to fill your heart with praise. It's being recorded heaven to earth. Let my love persuade you to be alive with joy!

Fountain of Life

See my love surround you. Your eyes are locked on mine. I send you the authority to love life in my midst. Your spirit is mine. Nowhere can compare to my compassion. My love lifts the lowest low and controls the highest high. Chatter in your ears will stop and be filled with praise from your mouth. The risk of doubt no longer exists because of an overwhelming increase of faith. Cry out to the Father for with his authority, we can direct the arm of God. He instructs us to. Do not be afraid; I am yours, and you are mine. Nothing can separate us.

Hunger Reigns

Spiritual hunger is alive. Seek the Lord's face. Empty your desires at his feet. Hunger to love his flock like he does. The one who is not clothed will be covered; the one who cannot see shall be given sight. So much hunger in sight. The one who has not been fed shall not starve. Because of his perfect hunger to fulfill needs. Shout praises in his name. Let the hungry ocean scream with joy! False hope shall be stopped. Love will endlessly pour out healing touch from the Holy Spirit.

Angels Are Coming

Look to the God of all to send his mighty forces of angels to rest in our presence. First, we will be in awe, then God will fill our hearts with glory. Worship is the authority delivered to us from God. Their wings have beauty. Glorious heavenly host, you are the King of glory. Shift the level of power to release the bondage. Nothing, absolutely nothing, can separate you from me! You are mine. My angels are yours.

Holy Spirit Clarity

I deliver you by my authority. I leave my hand on you with perfect peace. Use this authority with love and grace. You need not hide in your inability. I will pour my oil over you. Shout praises to the heavens. I will stop to listen and deliver you from your haste. Angels flutter their wings with my breath to send peace—real comfort deep to your core. Indescribable! Only the King of glory can capture your soul in freedom and purity.

Look to the Father

When all is good, look to the Father. He alone stabilizes our need. Do not shuffle your beliefs to worldly teachings. Take no other teaching other than my Word. It will always reign true! Holy Spirit comes to give peace and wisdom. Shout and speak through his anointing to crush the head of the enemy. Look for the face of God to teach you his mercies with love and compassion. Search for your spot in his realm. You should be guided by the Holy One.

Soaring with the Heavenly

When I look over the valley from the mountaintops, I soar like eagles with great flight. I feel the wind touch my soul by the hand of the Holy Spirit. My voice cries out. Let me go with your love to deliver you from darkness. Light brings the King of glory. Settle your power and authority and grace and anointing with God's love. Healings renew our minds. My bondage is gone; freedom is apparent. It is settled!

Seeking Choice

I'm waiting for you to ready my choice. I enter the quiet place to search the details of your heart, Father God. Choose the path to righteousness. Rest and grow in his delight. Enter the glory of worship with intensity. The dominion of sound will release your bondage and give you new peace so deep the angels will not have seen it. Choice is a God-given power attached to our free will. The Holy Spirit will cause us to do God's will. Choice is the Father's will.

Sacrifice Is the Rule

Give me your all, child. I will honor your sacrifice and turn it to love abounding with grace. Lose your withholding spirit. Give to me your most prized, precious gift. There is no sacrifice as great as mine. The Father's love gave his only begotten Son. Love is the ultimate sacrifice. Heal my wounds; let love consume me through and through. Eternal hope gives my spirit the ultimate sacrifice—love.

Holy Water of Time

Looking to your Spirit, O Father, and reaching to the innermost core of my being. Let it run from my heart into the world. Heavenly messages from ministering angels let loose the dominion of your power. Then comes the light to control the sound of worshipping angels. The whole earth will shake and tremble from that sound. The dominion of healing takes charge of all sickness and weakness of troubled spirits. Wipe all doubt from this planet to settle in glory from the Father forever, amen.

I Appeared to You

There was a form of an angel in my midst tracking me to my purpose. It slowed my being to check my motives.

"Just know you are loved; your abilities are mine. I created them just for you. I appeared to you so you would know my peace. Fear would fall to the ground, and love would take over. In my presence, you surrendered to my will. I delivered a gift to you and told you to use it—it's free from guilt and performance! Rest your spirit in my power with your praise and know that every time I hear it, I love you."

Rushing through the Meadow

Look to the heavens and see what God has created for you. LOVE is at hand to lift up your spirit and release his perfect love and peace. Settle what is uneasy with my glory to empower you to serve me. Cry out to my Holy Spirit, and he will bring you a well of living waters under your feet. Know the enemy must take his hands off of God's people and property. He has no business here. So when you open your eyes, there will be no fear cast. Just joy. My hand will hold you in your journey to my kingdom. With your faith, don't let the enemy fight you in isolation. Love is mighty and endlessly given by my power and my might. Use my Holy Spirit to drive out fear and live in freedom.

Seeing with Your Eyes

I look to the skies, and you show me your love in the clouds covered with angels. Send to me your vision. Search my thoughts; release the peace of the lilies growing in the quiet. Hold my thoughts in your palm. Shift my thinking to the heavenly realm.

Free me from the bondage of self. Go to my core and see with your eyes what causes resistance to your will. Never let me excuse your power and grace—only accept it with joy.

I'm a Reflection of Your Actions

Move into my presence. Seek my face, and I will honor your spirit, which I have installed in you. Birds will stop their flight to hear my voice. When you speak to me, my breath increases to bless you. Take action. Lay down your false stimulation. Pursue my joy brought by the Holy Spirit. Fall to my strength, and let your actions be consistent to true joy. Love is the catalyst to joy. Do not rest and be satisfied with yourself. I am your true revival. Celebrate Jesus for eternity!

Such a Voice!

What is that sound? It is an angel from the Lord looking for cooperation from your voice. "Search your inner spirit, lift up the Lord, and move the love in your hearts. Eyes are filled with glory to shift evil and move it out of his way. Enter the glory realm with intent to destroy the works of the enemy.

"Your worry is mine," says the Father.

"I have created you to be in my hands. You are my children forever. No one but me can destroy man."

Sensing Love

Sleeping in the night, I'm awakened sensing your love, Father God. I choose the real property of your power to direct me and my feet. Holy Spirit, I call on your love and power coming down from above. Teach my spirit to sense your love and tap into your power. I will PUSH (pray until something happens) with prayer.

Search your heart, and know who you are. Trust the love around you. Embrace it so you can install it in someone else. Let your praise go to worship and then to glory.

Knowing

It is beyond me that I can seek and reach God's power. But wait: God delivers his love without reserve. We must go to war with the prophecy personally given to us. Prophecies are words from God for you. Wage war with faith and a clean conscience. A divided conscience creates weak faith. Come to me as a child to receive your inheritance. Bone of bone, flesh of flesh. You are built from God. Take it by force to battle these prophecies. My family and I will live for the Lord. Go to war.

Host the Prophetic

Cast down the strongholds in your life. Each time we have depression, fear, lack, or negative thinking, put on the helmet of salvation. Think saved, not lies of the enemy. Don't let the enemy build a castle brick by brick. He has no power. Think salvation. Activate the prophecies in your house. Treasure the words of personal prophecies. When God speaks a prophecy over me, I take it out and wear it like fine jewelry. Angels hear God's words decreed. Don't stop your angels. Whosoever tells the mountains to move shall move mountains.

You Are a Child of Mine

It was decided by divine appointment who I was to be. Glorious thoughts reach out from the heavens. God knew who and what I would become even as I was a crying child in the dark. My value is held in his heart, the Father God. Nothing stops that perfect creation. God breathes his breath to seal his win. "Not by might nor by power, but by my will," sayeth the Lord. Bring me instruction on how to wait. Install your gifts from the Holy Spirit. I reach for you, my God. Let me touch and feel your presence. Teach me to listen with a perfect ear. Deliver through me the sound of praise.

Settle My Heart

Teach me to see beyond my external circumstances. To feel weak and abandoned is human. Look to your heart to identify those weaknesses. No amount of me can heal the damage within. I need Jesus to complete me. No more hauntings screaming in my ear. Your voice, God, is powerful. It took me to my knees asking Jesus to please comfort my inner core. Let me settle my heart in your perfect peace. Open my eyes to see your endless beauties. Broaden my faith so I'm not crushed. Let the Holy Spirit sing to my core. Make it unshakeable!

Pulled Up by the Roots

Shivering to my core in the darkness, I came to. Lost and alone. Suddenly an angel appeared, and I became very weak. Not knowing if he was from God, I asked him who sent him. "Am I going to live or die?" He said, "I am here to comfort you and rest with you while you seek the Father."

I began to weep; I knew I wouldn't die. That angel delivered hope to me, which caused me to get pulled up by the roots from the power of the Father God.

Shadows on the Edge

I look around me and see shadows nurturing me all around. I open my voice to receive the glory. I run out of the shadows to the light, wash in the glory; make endless sounds to shift the darkness and lose the chains that bind me. Hiding in the shadows is the authority to operate in the Holy Ghost. He gives you value and holds your bondage so you are not trapped. Search the levels of your edge so you don't fall. Trust Jesus to hold you true to heart. No uncontrollable fear to send you to doubt. "Know that I am the Lord."

Sure-footed

I am resting in the loft with sure-footed angels. I see the land God has made with his mighty hand. My peace is flowing like a mellow brook. First one foot, then the other. I feel firmly planted in the kingdom with the heavenly Father. There is no shaking or soft ground under my feet—only angels all around.

"Call me by name and know that I am your God, sure-footed, tempered, and true. You see, it's not about the soil. It's about the seed, so be sure-footed and love like me."

Wanting Spirit

Wake to my presence, seek my face, be bold when you speak in love concerning the Holy Spirit. It is holiness that surrounds the caliber of loveliness to rein in eternity, giving always to those who receive with willingness. Search the platform and know his mighty voice when it whispers in the secret place that he has given you. Know that what is silent makes a heavenly sound. No bearer will stop your request. Desire is filled with authority and power. You are in full flight with angels resting.

Mighty Breath of God

You fill my lungs with power and grace. Let me search the heavens to feel your mighty breath across on my face. This breath carries healing and great peace. The angels bow on bended knees for this breath riddled with pain. It carried release of bondage. The chains are broken; the key is turned with his mighty breath. Shake the boughs of the trees; let the birds fly and soar to heaven with the grace of his breath. Then streams of mercy float on his breath to seal his glory in our souls.

Foundation of Freedom

On bended knee, I asked you to free me from the bondage of self. My request was honored with no hesitation. The Father said, "Yes! Yes! I have always held you in my arms! The planet may waver; however, I will not. This foundation is my love served to your spirit to dance in grace and mercy. Freedom comes in the form of free will to only you, my human race. Choose to worship me and rest in the glory. Fear must go! It can't live in the presence of the Holy Spirit!"

I Hold You Dear

My darling child, you are worth every effort to develop your abilities to the Father. Sweet air is the source of the Father's breath. Teach me to receive your most high blessing. Rest in the glory so I can have the power to do creative miracles. Laugh with the love of the Holy Spirit. Search the stars for a story to be told. Speak truth and be earnest about my actions. Live for the purpose of the heavenly Father. Serve the needy of heart, love the children, dance in the spirit, and win the nations.

Balance Your Spirit

Enter into the perpetual quietness of the Holy Spirit. Come into complete agreement to find spiritual balance. Rest in the Father's arms. Angels are on assignment to bring confirmation to balance our spirits. Only the voice of the Holy Spirit is heard—no counterfeits. Take all vexations off my spirit. Release your power, Father God. Thank you for your Son and all of his works. Living waters permeate my pores with divine love, knowing that I am a child of the Most High King who paid the ransom for me.

Harmony Mindset

Release heaven to my mind. Let eternity dwell in the midst of my being. Lose the warring angels to protect the innocence of our hearts. Let our eyes see color like flowing liquid. Rest the wings of the birds; stop all creation in your presence. Let us harmonize our core to your sounds, your voice, your touch. Holiness is upon us to release your power and grace, love not equal to any. Put a touch in my hands for your abilities to be used as your gifts. Heal the broken, and free the captive.

Source of Power

I enter on my knees to humble my spirit, not driven by ego or circumstance but submissive obedience to God the Father. I feel the power in the glory; the hand of the Father is within my spirit. I call on the angels to stand watch and carry messages recovered back to heaven. Walk in love and grace. Receive forgiveness and give forgiveness to be released into freedom. Unlock spiritual captivity. Crush the enemy with the blood of Jesus. By his stripes, we are healed. Rebuke the devil for he has no hold on God's children!

Magnified Love

I am seeing the source of love. It's flowing through my veins. I feel your love stopping my selfish tales, which bind me tightly so that I am not free. Absorb my motives and turn them to your love; undo the hardness of my fleshly heart, and put a blanket of your love to block the enemy. Magnify the ability to love unconditionally and worship with the Holy Spirit. Speak to magnify his love on the whole earth; peace be still. Quietly loving all things with the power of the Most High God, let my first report be of his magnified love touching every living soul.

I Shall Rejoice in My People

By my spirit, I will have the victory. By my spirit, I open the eyes of the blind. For surely, I shall move, and no hand shall stop me. I will break through the locked gates as a flow of flaming lava. I will not withhold my power and my glory from any seeking heart. They who desire me, I will surely reward. I will not fail. I will fill every longing heart and satisfy every craving soul. My grace will pour out as a tumbling waterfall. I shall be glorified. I shall be magnified. And I will rejoice in my people when they yield themselves free from everything else. Then I shall cast my love above them as a cloak. And I will whisper my words in their ears.

Lean into My Power

Lean so far that your faith is pulled off the shelf. Work in the Holy Spirit. It's all about you. The gifts that he gave to you are fully activated. I sense the power coming down from above. Angels sent to deliver messages from the Father are clearly spoken and dearly heard. Raise your voice and lean into my power, sight unseen. Faith wiggles all doubt out of my soul. I believe in the power of God, and he's one hundred percent when you're on the edge. He lets me lean into his power for freedom, mercy, and grace.

A Loving Word

God has put me among some of his loving students to impart to me their knowledge and love through Christ and the Holy Spirit. Their voices are likened to power and willingness. They are teachable and pursue the Father's love. A helping spirit lends encouragement to fellow students. Kindness is a living presentation of God's grace living in you. We walk to Jesus with our actions and voices. He hears us and enlightens us, opens our eyes and ears so he can speak to us clearly about his grace and how he never stops thinking of us.

Forever Thirsty

Drink from the holy waters flowing in the Holy Spirit. Send echoes of love through your voices. Know that Jesus loves you and carried all your weakness under the mighty arm of God. The thirst deepens as I follow directions from the angel sent to fulfill my thirst. Roam to the beat of heaven's song; all the land will listen to it and be thirsty for more! The living water flows through the rocks, and they come alive with the glory that is heaven-sent. Rest and be fervent.

Be of Good Spirit

Happy are ye who seek the Lord. Trust in him; he will provide and fulfill your desires. Be of good cheer; sound off to the heavens. Let the angels hear the joy of your heart. Rattle fear's structure built by the devil. He will flee, and fear will surround him. The voice of the Holy Spirit will stop him in his tracks. Expose his tricks and follies. Let faith be strong and full to overcome weakness. Good spirit is the resounding heartfelt cry to the heavens. Angels will rejoice with love.

Our Father

Dear heavenly Father, open my heart to your love. Surround me with your presence. Leave me wanting your touch. If only I could ready my spirit for your power and glory on an every-moment basis. Let me seek your face and see what is in your will. Oh, our Father, you truly love me to no end. When I look to the sky, your hand touches my spirit, and it flutters like the wings of a hummingbird. Release your power and justice for your purpose. Always to end fear and replace it with love.

Counseled by the Holy Spirit

When I awake, I am greeted by holy breath. It is the Holy Spirit. Upon request, I'm stalled, and take time to harmonize with the Father in his glory. I dance, I sing, I laugh, I cry. Every sound I hear is God's voice through the Holy Spirit. Carry me to the will of my heavenly Father. Jesus, set me free, guide my steps to the water, wash my hardness off of me. Remove the shell of this world, and let me be free. Free to have your peace in me. Deliver more power, more peace. Rest in your love, see with the eyes of an eagle. Let angels sing.

Breaking the Course of Failure

I reach for the Holy Spirit, and he warms my heart. Let the angels surround my being and deliver messages from heaven. Father God, you are my source. I can trust no other. You set a constant course for my soul headed to you and your promised land. Let me seek always your will. I cannot fail. Jesus, you are my navigation. The line you set for me is strong and unshakeable. Oh, evil, you don't stand a chance. Holy fire will consume you! It is glory and God's power that holds the course to his path of love.

God Sees Mercy

Father, you are the God of mercy. Love is the directive in our hearts. Let your strength be our foundation. We serve you to the point of sacrifice and beyond. Change everything in me that is not of you, Father God. Search my heart and pull out the brokenness and seal your love to a high degree. Push me to your presence and cause me to seek your face. May angels show me your signs and deliver to me your will without doubt. Let me fall into your arms and praise your name. Release me from my prison so I can bring your love to the captive. Let me draw near to your Holy Spirit. I want to please you and not do my will. O God, speak to me, open my ears. O God, reveal to me and open my eyes. O God, open my eyes, remove the scales, launch in me your heavenly freedom.

Seen on Higher Ground

Looking to the Holy Spirit, I see my weakness in glory. Such is the way of his power. Reaching to the lowest valleys to bring us to higher ground, the eyes of God are upon us. Worthy is he! Lost forever, he found us and bought our souls with a ransom of his blood. Work to be his servant. Let loose that which binds me. Leave me not in the desert. Sow into me your goodness and compassion. Rattle the enemy to his worthless bones. Cause him to run and hide. Father God, you love us to the degree that is indescribable. I believe what you say about me. Say who I am. I need to know and repeat to others in the power of my testimony. It is you, Father, Son, and Holy Ghost, that I give the credit.

Left in Perfect Peace

I stood alone in perfect peace and heard the sound of angels rejoicing. Worship is at hand to let loose my spirit. Love conquered my turmoil. Suddenly, I was lost in the presence of my God. Peace is a powerful healing for my soul, and I am not consumed by my feelings of inadequacy. The power of the Holy Spirit left me suspended in perfect peace. Father, I ask you to empower your angels to deliver your peace. Let my humanness be overridden by your hand. Cause perfect peace to shatter the scream of the enemy. Bring the Spirit gifting into the room. Move, Holy Spirit. Let us respond to your commands. Hallelujah!

Searching for Passion

To the one who sees my face, I shall hear your cries. Test the waters; they are pure and transparent. Lose the terrifying fear that shreds my spirit. O Father God, let your grace humble me to your presence, seeking the peace you promised me. I know you can't lie, so I'll believe you and honor you with my faith. Teach me your living Word— sew it into my DNA. Live in the reign of glory. Send angels to the earth to deliver messages to your people. Search the corners of my heart for light and healing brought about through passion that is the Holy Spirit. Create in me the vision to see holy function and direction. Let the spectrum of light be brilliant to direct the path for angel armies. All praises to the Father God, the Holy One!

Waves of Glory

Enter my core and cleanse the human depravity and bring your holiness. Let it vibrate through my spirit until my body overflows with it. Heal all the wounds that the enemy left in me to cause me to die spiritually. Awaken the living Holy Spirit in me to reign with power and grace. Let honor direct my path to righteousness. Seek to love and let Jesus boast healing about your people. The angels of the east, west, north, and south create in me a servant's heart. Let me prefer you, Jesus, over everything else. I call on you to deliver, set free, and settle the wrongs of the enemy. Because I have put my hand on you, they will know it is I in you. Look, it is the living God!

Comfort in the Glory

Entering into praise with my heart wide open, I am settled with a warming in my spirit. Touched by his love, all is clear to wake the consuming glory. Trust his powerful delivery of peace, so overwhelming when I feel his spirit washing over me. Lost to this realm, I now enter the realm of the glory. It's a great cloud completely covering me. My eyes are closed to the power. Fear flees, and joy enters my heart. The vast glory brings spiritual comfort to my very core. This glory allows me to rest in the face of Jesus. Such beauty and grace! Complete freedom.

Visions of Delight

Oh, breath of God, breathe on me. Send your glorious delight in a vision to open the airwaves. Make me a pillar of your power. Release your Holy Ghost into the airways. Let angels fly to their destination to protect the weak and fallen. Overturn broken homes, and heal the land. Release your living word in truth. Let the babbling words of deceit be crushed by your truth. Loud noises from heaven are heard through formerly deaf ears. You cast out demons and darkness, then light takes over. God, through Jesus the Son, empowered by the Holy Spirit, is at work here.

River's Edge

Look to the running waters of the river. See it carry cleansing ability. Compare its great force with that of God and know he created the river and its edge. It's capable of cutting rock and other hard substances like the human heart. The edge of the river is cut with soft edges. Lose the grains of sand as Father God has already counted them. The river's edge has a song so loved and pure it is directed by angels. Receive the Father's glory and power. May the Holy Spirit open all the block of unbelief. Crush the devil and all his allies. The heavenly holds the edge.

Spirit Blessings

Father God, I bless their spirit with your truth and power infused with the Holy Spirit. Let their choice be Jesus the Son. Enter their being and teach your unconditional love. Search the dark corners of their hearts and illuminate them with light. Walk hand in hand with their hands. Set a fire deep in their souls. Let living waters cleanse their minds and adapt to the mind of Christ. May angels be on assignment to them. Protection from your heavenly holiness permeates my spirit.

The Effect of Holy Power

See the drop of love on the ocean as the waves reach magnitudes of healing. The power does not stop. Teach us to bring your love, Father God, to the water of the Holy Spirit. It is by your power and grace that you sew into our lives. Let us run to the rain when it falls. Grow our faith so we can please you. Touch our cores until they respond to all of your creation. Set your sights on Christ. Become his bond servant. Let him direct your love to new highs. Reach the unreachable, and let the power of God touch them.

Sense of Peace

Look to my spirit, and touch my soul. Bring peace in, and let it rest. Search my heart, and look for fear. I command fear to go! Do not let this fear create a spiritual wasteland. Heavenly waters carried by angels are poured out on my head. The blessing of oil establishes a sense of peace in our spirits. Rush through waves of glory. Father God sends heavenly peace to pass all understanding. Let your fire fly to us. Deliver your verbal peace and external commands. Rest in peace.

Over and Over

Over and over, your love stands strong.
Over and over, your power reigns.
Over and over, your grace saves!
Over and over, your peace saves me.
Over and over, your healing touches me.
Over and over, you recreate in me a new fresh spirit.
Over and over, you reveal yourself to me.
Over and over, you give to me freedom!

Finally, God

Dear heavenly Father, you bless me endlessly. You give to me the abilities to be more powerful than angels. You open my eyes to look at what is real. You warm my heart with great love beyond comprehension. You let loose my spirit to be in unity with you. Your Holy Spirit causes me to dance like I was a wild bird looking for a safe landing. Pick up all of your gifts, and display your beauty and power. Your mighty hand holds the entire universe still to teach and share your greatness for eternity!

"Victory Will Be Mine," Sayeth the Lord!

By my Spirit, I will have the victory. By my Spirit, I will open the eyes of the blind. For surely I will move, and no hand shall stop me. I will break through the locked gates as a flow of flaming lava.

I will not withhold my power and my glory from any seeking heart. They who have a passion for me I will surely reward. I will not fail. I will fill every longing heart and satisfy every craving soul. My grace will pour out as a tumbling waterfall. I shall be glorified. I shall be magnified. And I will rejoice in my people when they yield themselves free from everything else. Then I shall cast my love about them as a cloak. And I will whisper my words in their ear.

About the Author

The author of this book is a Spirit-filled Christian husband, father, and grandpa. He is in tune with the Holy Spirit and God's Word and wants the world to know Jesus's love.

CPSIA information can be obtained
at www.ICGtesting.com
Printed in the USA
FSHW010842181121
86267FS